W9-BWM-377

Pitcairn Island
refuge of
The Bounty Mutineers

Maurice Allward

Christian's Cave. This has a commanding view of the open sea and is now a popular venue for visitors to Pitcairn Island.

PITCAIRN ISLAND
REFUGE OF
THE BOUNTY MUTINEERS

Maurice Allward

Dedicated to:
The islanders of Pitcairn who for two
centuries have given conjecture to
historians and pleasure to people all
over the world

TEMPUS

First published 2000
Copyright © Maurice Allward, 2000

Tempus Publishing Limited
The Mill, Brimscombe Port,
Stroud, Gloucestershire, GL5 2QG

ISBN 0 7524 1746 0

Typesetting and origination by
Tempus Publishing Limited
Printed in Great Britain by
Midway Clark Printing, Wiltshire

Acknowledgements

It is not possible to thank all those who provided help with this book. However, special thanks must go to the following descendents of the mutineers of the *Bounty* and Captain Bligh:

Wayne Adams, Bernard Christian-Bailey, Maurice Bligh, Brenda Christian, Olive Christian, Steve Christian and Ross Quintal.

Kind thanks are also given to the following individuals who gave generous help:
Carolyne Allward, Walter Bersinger, Murray Brown, Pam Brown, Thelma Brown, Sam Bryant, Paul Burnett, Peter Clarke, Gail Cox, Ron Edwards, Pauline Ernst, Clive Farahar, Anthony Fisher, Lord Gainford, Jerry Gordon, Len Hartley, Geoffrey Hubbard, Anders Kallgard, Douglas Lawrence (Pitcairn Island family tree specialist), Austin Meares, Spencer Murray (*Pitcairn Island – The First Two Hundred Years*), Bryant Moon, John O'Conner, Max Pudney, David Ransom, Fred and Nan Smith, Jeff Thomas, Jay Warren, Tim Waters and Moira Winner.

Thanks are also due to many companies, including:
Bonhams Auctioneers, Bounty Cruises, Bounty Folk Museum, Bounty Sagas, Christie's Auctioneers, George Prior Engineering, Fiji Museum, National Maritime Museum, Norfolk Island Historical Society, Pitcairn Island Philatelic Bureau, Pitcairn Miscellany, Royal New Zealand Air Force and the State Library of New South Wales, Sydney, all of whom allowed their photographs to be used free of charge.

Very special thanks must go to my long suffering wife Joy, who gave up the use of her dining-room table for three years while this book was being prepared.

Contents

His Majesty's Armed Vessel *Bounty*. A true to scale replica made for the 1984 Orion Pictures film of the mutiny, starring Mel Gibson and Anthony Hopkins.

Introduction

On 23 December 1787 a small, three-masted ship sailed from Spithead on the south coast of England. This was the beginning of a voyage which has become world famous over the passing of two centuries. The name of the ship was the *Bounty*, and the name of her commander was William Bligh. One member of his crew of forty-five, a close friend, was a young sailor named Fletcher Christian. All three names play a key part in the story of the voyage.

The purpose of the voyage was to collect breadfruit plants from the island of Tahiti in the middle of the Pacific Ocean, and then to transport them to the West Indies to grow and provide food for slaves working on the plantations. Although long, the voyage was not expected to be especially arduous, apart from the order, having secured the cargo of breadfruit, to sail for the dangerous Endeavour Strait (now known as the Torres Strait) round the north-eastern tip of Australia, and chart a navigable route to the East Indies.

A small vessel was bought by the British Admiralty especially for the voyage. This was the *Bethia*, originally built to carry coal. When converted to carry breadfruit plants, it was classified as an armed transport and thus officially referred to as HMAV – His Majesty's Armed Vessel *Bounty*, the new name given to the ship after conversion. The *Bounty* was 91ft long, had a beam of 24ft and weighed 215 tons. Being designed to carry coal it had well-rounded bilges, enabling it to remain upright on the muddy banks of rivers in England, as well as on the sandy shores of distant islands. To accommodate many hundreds of plants the great cabin was specially adapted, which significantly reduced the living space for the crew.

The *Bounty* and her crew had been ready for the voyage for over a month before the Admiralty issued the order for it to leave. This delay is considered by some as the initial reason for the later tragedies. Even if there had not been a mutiny, reaching the treacherous Torres Strait out of season could have been disastrous. A month of good sailing weather was lost, and soon after leaving port the *Bounty* encountered fierce gales that caused serious damage to the ship, equipment and stores. To repair the damage and restock the supplies, Bligh took the *Bounty* to Puerto de la Cruz in Tenerife, causing further delay.

Early in the voyage Bligh instituted the first of many procedures indicative of the care and consideration he had for the crew. To improve conditions on board the cramped ship he split the customary 'watches' into three, instead of the usual two, to provide periods of unbroken sleep, plus time for relaxation.

An early painting showing the Bounty *taking on stores at Portsmouth in 1787.*

Another indication of Bligh's concern for the well-being of his crew who, incidentally, were all volunteers, not press-ganged, was the enlistment of Michael Byrne as a fiddler. He had very poor eyesight and therefore was not able to undertake normal able seaman's duties. His job was to play music during the months of sailing to which the crew jigged to keep fit. Often there were long periods sailing with the trade winds, when there was little work to do.

Countering the benefits of such considerate actions, however, was Bligh's abusive language and sarcastic criticism of both his officers and deck crew. Even in an age when bad language at sea was the norm, it was foul and demoralizing. Also, Bligh often shouted and swore at his senior men in the hearing of those of lower rank, which was not likely to improve their loyalty, even when they may have deserved a dressing down. Bligh had a quick temper and after an outburst would behave as if nothing had happened. His words, however, were not as quickly forgotten by those who were the object of his anger.

Bligh's orders from the Admiralty were that he should try and get to Tahiti by taking the 'short' route round the Horn of South America. Due to the inexplicable delay in leaving England, Bligh knew that this would be even more difficult than normal because of the lateness of the season and consequent bad weather. In the event it proved impossible.

However, Bligh, his crew and the sturdy *Bounty* tried their very best. For thirty-one days there were terrible storms and the crew faced great danger and hardship. During the attempted passage driving rain, hail, sleet and raging seas washed over the deck and poured down the hatchways. It was during this difficult period that Bligh proved what a great commander he could be. Under his orders the crew worked magnificently, and the little *Bounty* did not lose a single spar or yard of canvas. Contributing to the performance of the *Bounty* was that it carried less ballast than normal and had had its mainmast shortened. Asking for this to be done when the ship was being converted, Bligh remarked that it would make the ship safer in really rough seas.

The trying period provided yet another example of the concern Bligh had for the welfare of his crew. To ease the hardship of those working on the main deck, he gave orders that the men below should ensure that there was dry, warm clothing and hot food waiting for the others when they came down below. This service was possible due to Bligh's foresight in purchasing, at his own expense, coal for the ship's stove, for which the Admiralty had made little or no provision. Bligh considered that the weather around Cape Horn would be extremely cold and commented 'without proper heating below decks, my men will not be able to stand it'.

Forced at last to turn around, the *Bounty* proceeded east across the South Atlantic, and on 25 May arrived at False Bay near Cape Town, in South Africa. There the little ship was repaired while the crew regained their health. The refurbished *Bounty* was then steered eastwards across the Indian Ocean and along the southern coast of Australia to Adventure Bay in Van Dieman's Land (now Tasmania). This leg was the longest of the voyage, 6,000 miles, and was sailed as a straight line. It is one of the world's great examples of accurate navigation. Halfway along the perfect straight line is St Paul's Rock, a tiny barren speck poking up out of the Indian Ocean, which was sighted as the *Bounty* passed close by.

Tahiti was finally reached on 26 October 1788 and the *Bounty* dropped its anchor in Matavai Bay. The Tahitians had spotted the vessel as soon as it was visible on the horizon, and were ready with their customary warm and friendly greetings. They swarmed about the ship in their double-hulled canoes and outriggers. The *Bounty* had reached its destination after a voyage of 27,086 miles, lasting ten months.

Once on Tahiti Bligh lost no time in implementing the object of the voyage – the collection of breadfruit plants. On board the *Bounty* were many items of great interest and value to the Tahitians, notably axes, knives and other metal implements. Bligh knew the district chief from an earlier visit with that great explorer of the time, Captain Cook, and was in fact revered as Captain Cook's son. He distributed gifts and cleverly steered the negotiations until the Tahitians asked what sort of gift they could send to King George III in return, making several suggestions. When they mentioned breadfruit, Bligh said that it would be a fine offering.

Perhaps the major consequence of the Admiralty delay in issuing the order for the *Bounty* to leave England was now to become evident, but not for the reason often given – that the late arrival meant that the season for collecting breadfruit was over. This was not so. Breadfruit trees and saplings of various kinds were available all the year round, and the quantity required could have been gathered in two or three weeks. The most time-consuming task would have been the repair and refurbishment of the weatherworn *Bounty*, but even this was not the main reason for the actual stay of nearly six months.

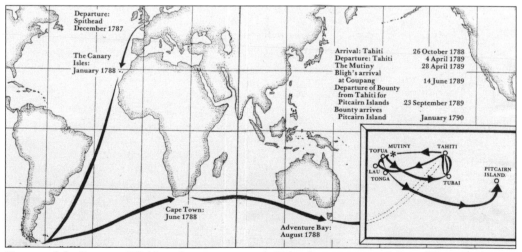

Voyage of the Bounty. *Bligh's orders were to reach Tahiti by going around Cape Horn. Because of severe storms this proved impossible, and the ship was turned eastward, reaching the island by way of Cape Town and Adventure Bay in Tasmania.*

Breadfruit. Easy to grow and nutritious, the task of the Bounty was to collect breadfruit plants in Tahiti and take them to the West Indies for use as food for slaves on plantations. The Bounty trip was unsuccessful, but later, when breadfruit was eventually transported to the West Indies, the slaves would not eat it. Today, however, breadfruit is the staple diet of many islands in the Caribbean.

The prime reason was that the late arrival in Tahiti meant that the hurricane season was approaching, making sailing in that part of the Pacific very hazardous. In particular, to return early would have meant that the *Bounty* would have encountered violent winds blowing from the west along the Torres Strait, through which the Admiralty wanted Bligh to sail. At that time such a journey would have been almost impossible, as was the earlier attempt to round the Horn 'out of season'. So the return had to be delayed until the promise of better weather.

The *Bounty* crew did not object. Tahiti was a paradise on earth for western sailors. The weather was warm and pleasant, fresh fruit could be plucked easily from trees, and the sea teemed with fish. Life was very easy compared with the cramped conditions on board the *Bounty* and the harsh realities of life at that time in far-away England. Perhaps the greatest attraction of all was the beautiful, sun-tanned, seductive Tahitian women.

The long stay in the lovely tropical conditions of Tahiti was certainly a catalyst for the later mutiny. With the advantage of hindsight it is now often suggested that Bligh should have ensured the maintenance of skills and discipline among his crew, for example, by taking the *Bounty* out regularly for short trips. However, such absences of the ship would have upset the delicate political situation. Having the *Bounty* offshore of people friendly to Bligh, as opposed to those of other chiefs, gave the Matavai Bay people a distinct feeling of one-upmanship.

With little work to do ashore many of the crew formed close, amorous relationships with their female companions. Christian, for example, set up home with one who has been described as the loveliest of the many pretty girls available. Often referred to as a daughter of one of the island chiefs, her name was Mauatua. Later Christian changed it to Isabella, the name of a former first cousin back home, of whom he was very fond, and had hoped to marry. The English maiden, however, had turned him down and instead married another cousin. Naturally, Christian was very upset by the rejection. Until then he had been training for a career in the law, but within six months he had gone to sea. Another name often given to Mauatua was

Mainmast, because, it is said, of her manner of standing very upright. Others called her Maimiti.

Several incidents marred the basic tranquillity of life ashore, as indeed similar incidents had marred the visits of ships before the *Bounty*. Isaac Martin, an able seaman, was given nineteen lashes for hitting a native. Alexander Smith and Muspratt were lashed for neglecting duties, and Thompson was punished for insolence and disobedience.

However, under the skilful guidance of David Nelson, the gardener, breadfruit plants were carefully and steadily nurtured until, with over one thousand on board, the *Bounty* left Tahiti on 4 April 1789 for the West Indies.

There is little doubt that many members of the crew, if they had been allowed to, would have elected to stay on the magic island, where they had formed close bonds with their Tahitian companions. In fact, three members of the crew, Muspratt, Millward and Churchill, had already stolen one of the *Bounty's* boats and some muskets, and deserted during the previous January. However, they were soon rounded up, through information given by island chiefs to Bligh. For this escapade Churchill received twelve lashes, and his two companions twenty-four lashes each. They were then kept in irons and three weeks later the punishments were repeated, after which they were released. These punishments may seem brutal and harsh today, but by the standards of that time they were very light. Each of the three crimes committed, stealing a boat, taking firearms and deserting, were capital offences, so the punishments ordered by Bligh were only a token of what they could have been. When six men had deserted another captain a little earlier, three were hanged, two were given 500 lashes and one 200 lashes.

The lack of success of these deserters may have given others something to think about. It was obvious that to desert by walking away or rowing a short distance would not succeed. The white man's hiding place would soon be given away by local natives. To get to a place of safety, and have protection from hostile natives, they would need a large, well-defended vessel – the *Bounty*. The possibility of taking the ship may thus have been discussed in hushed voices even

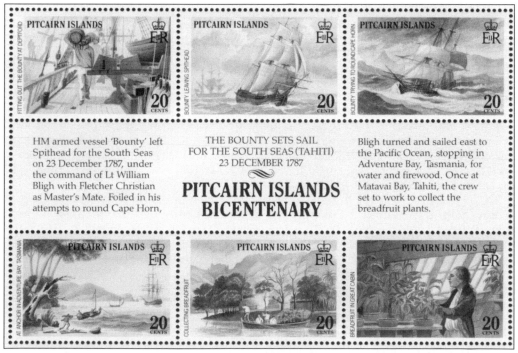

The story of the mutiny on the Bounty was well told on a series of commemorative stamps issued by Pitcairn Island in 1989. These six stamps show scenes of the Bounty leaving England, the ship at Cape Horn and the crew collecting breadfruit plants.

The stamps bear the following text:

PITCAIRN ISLANDS E·R — 90 CENTS *(BOUNTY LEAVING MATAVAI BAY)*

PITCAIRN ISLANDS E·R — 90 CENTS *(THE MUTINY – BLIGH BEING AWOKEN)*

PITCAIRN ISLANDS E·R — 90 CENTS *(CONFRONTATION BETWEEN BLIGH & CHRISTIAN)*

After a five month stay at Matavai Bay, Tahiti, where the crew collected breadfruit plants, HMAV 'Bounty' sailed for the West Indies on 4 April 1789. Twenty-four days later, near Tonga, some of the crew

THE MUTINY
ON THE BOUNTY
28 APRIL 1789

**PITCAIRN ISLANDS
BICENTENARY**

mutinied. Lieutenant Bligh, with eighteen seamen, was set adrift in an open boat and 'Bounty', with the mutineers led by Fletcher Christian, sailed off to find a safe refuge.

PITCAIRN ISLANDS E·R — 90 CENTS *(BLIGH BEING FORCED INTO OPEN BOAT)*

PITCAIRN ISLANDS E·R — 90 CENTS *(CASTING ADRIFT OF BLIGH)*

PITCAIRN ISLANDS E·R — 90 CENTS *(THROWING BREADFRUIT PLANTS OVERBOARD)*

A second set of commemorative stamps issued by Pitcairn in 1989. These include pictures of the Bounty leaving Tahiti, the mutiny and Bligh being cast adrift. The last stamp shows the mutineers throwing breadfruit plants overboard.

before the ship left the island. Such thoughts would have been encouraged by the fact that the *Bounty* was an unguarded expeditionary ship.

In an effort to restore the efficiency of his out-of-practice crew, Bligh used – according to some crew members, but not all – even more violent language, with dire threats of what would happen if they did not perform their duties properly. According to him they were all 'scoundrels, rascals, hell hounds, beasts and infamous wretches'.

Much of this invective was directed against Christian, who was already depressed about leaving his beautiful Mauatua behind. Also, he was possibly unwell. To overcome a skin disease he was taking laudanum from the ship's medical chest as a painkiller, but the supply had run out. Laudanum is a solution of opium, and without it he could have been suffering from the torment and anguish associated with withdrawal.

Christian seems to have finally broken down and lost control of his reason during what has become known as 'the coconut affair'. Although all food and stores on board were officially part of the *Bounty* provisions, nearly everyone had what he considered his own supply, and Bligh had his personal pile by the guns on deck. He suddenly turned to Christian and his watch crew shouting 'Damn your blood you have stolen my coconuts'. Christian, who had been on watch, at once admitted that he had taken one as he had been thirsty. Bligh then accused him of stealing half of them, yelling at the rest of the crew 'I'll make half of you jump overboard before you get through the Endeavour Strait!' Bligh's pile may well have become smaller during the night, as the crew would have trodden on it as they moved along the deck, but this explanation did not calm Bligh.

Although a long-time friend of Bligh, Christian could take his insults and denigration no longer, and planned to make a small raft and float away to the nearest island. He confided his plan to his friend Midshipman Young, who told him that the idea would not work, and would almost certainly result in his death, either by drowning, sharks or hostile natives.

Young is then thought to have told Christian that several other members of the crew wanted to desert. The promise of an end to the hard life at sea and a return to his loved one on a recently-left island paradise was too great a temptation. With their help Christian took over the chests housing the muskets, and then took control of the *Bounty*. Christian could, of course, have had such a plan in his mind long before the actual mutiny.

Bligh was woken, seized and brought up on deck, where preparations were made to set him adrift in the small cutter stowed on board. This was not only rotten, but too small, and instead the 23ft launch was slung overboard. Twelve people actively supported Christian; the remaining thirty or so wanted to accompany Bligh. The launch was far too small for this number and several were forced to remain on board. Bligh and eighteen others were cast adrift in a boat designed to carry twelve.

They were nearly four thousand miles from the nearest friendly territory, with no firearms and little food and water. They were being sent to almost certain death. However, against all the odds, losing only one man (to hostile natives) and after a voyage lasting forty-seven days, Bligh reached Coupang, a Dutch settlement in East Timor. This open-boat voyage, the longest ever made by a serving British naval officer, is remarkable for the leadership and navigational skill shown by Bligh, and the courage, resilience and determination of his crew. It has no equal in the long history of sea-faring.

Meanwhile, on the *Bounty* Christian was elected captain. His first inclination was to return to Tahiti to be reunited with friends. However, he knew that sooner or later British naval vessels would be sent to search for the *Bounty*, and decided to find another island as refuge. He chose Tubuai, a few hundred miles to the south-east, off the regular track of sailing vessels. Although the island had plenty of fruit, there was no livestock and after three days the *Bounty* sailed for Tahiti for supplies.

Restocked, the *Bounty* returned to Tubuai, where the crew hoped to build a permanent settlement. But the natives proved extremely hostile, due largely to the competing jealousies of local chiefs. After weeks of fighting, while the mutineers attempted to build 'Fort George', the idea was abandoned, and the *Bounty* was once again steered towards Tahiti to pick up friends, but also to get rid of the significant number of loyal men on board who had not mutinied and who might try and regain control of the ship. At Tahiti goods were divided equally between

An impression of the Bounty *launch in heavy sea with Bligh and eighteen loyal sailors on board. The 3,600 mile, forty-eight day voyage to Timor brought out the best of Bligh, as a commander and superb navigator, and illustrated the crew members' bravery and determination.*

The Bounty *near Pitcairn Island with the crew looking intently for any signs of life. A landing party later confirmed that it was uninhabited and that there were supplies of water and fruit.*

those who would stay on the island, and those who would leave with Christian. The *Bounty* was patched up and restocked yet again. Then, with Christian and eight fellow mutineers, six native men and twelve Tahitian women, a baby and hundreds of animals, the ship left the island for the fourth and last time.

For weeks the *Bounty* sailed the vast expanse of the great South Sea, now known as the Pacific Ocean, looking for a suitable island. Many were sighted, but only one was visited. This was Rarotonga, some 700 miles south-west of Tahiti and one of the most spectacularly beautiful Polynesian islands. But it was densely populated and clearly no place for the settlement of the mutineers.

The *Bounty* set sail once again. This time Christian was aiming for a tiny, distant island he had spotted on one of the charts in Bligh's cabin. Two months passed without any land being sighted. The men and women on board became discouraged, the latter in particular suffering from the previously inexperienced cold, due to the low latitude.

Just as they were giving up all hope, a tiny speck was sighted on the horizon. This was the island of Pitcairn. It had been discovered by Captain Carteret of HMS *Swallow* in 1767 and named after the young Midshipman, Robert Pitcairn, the first member of the crew to spot the island. Owing to the difficulty of determining longitude accurately at that time, its position was recorded inaccurately.

Thus, although appearing on Admiralty charts, it was shown about 200 miles to the west of its true position. It could therefore only be found by chance using the charts. It seemed to be the ideal refuge for the nine mutineers and the nineteen Polynesians they had brought with them.

The coastline of Pitcairn Island consists almost entirely of steeply rising cliffs, pounded by heavy seas, with only one small area for possible, but highly hazardous, landing. It is known today as Bounty Bay, but in those days the approach was dotted with rocks, which obviously had to be avoided. Landings were only possible in calm weather, and the mutineers were fortunate that their arrival coincided with a short period of calm sea.

The *Bounty* was run close inshore and tethered to a large tree. There followed a period of intense activity when everything of possible use, tools, sails, rope, the ship's anvil and a vice was removed. Wood from the decks and partitions was prised away and floated or carried ashore. Also taken were all the cooking utensils, barrels, boxes, livestock, plants, and nails, together with the muskets, powder, balls and cutlasses. Little Sarah, only ten months old and the youngest person on board, is said to have been pushed ashore inside a barrel.

Once ashore the material and stores had to be carried up the steep cliff facing the little beach, to the top where the terrain levelled off and was screened by trees. The way up the cliff was little more than a goat track and it was a real feat of endurance for the mutineers and their Tahitian companions to manhandle everything to the top. With good reason the track became known as the 'Hill of Difficulty'. It remained a major difficulty for over 150 years. As late as 1921 the British Government sent an official party to report on conditions on the island. The party landed, but the hill proved too steep and narrow for some members, who had to return to their ship without carrying out the survey.

Although much equipment was taken ashore, it seems that before this task could be completed the *Bounty* was set on fire accidentally. This was the fate that was planned, so that it would never be found, and also to prevent any possibility of anyone trying to take it back to England, or anywhere else, and so reveal the location of the colony. While on board McCoy found a bottle of liquor and became intoxicated. Dropping a match, the bone-dry ship readily caught fire and burned fiercely.

The thoughts of the watching mutineers on shore can only be imagined. Some, particularly Fletcher Christian, probably regretted their rash act of mutiny. All of them knew that never again would they see their native land, their parents or loved ones back home. They were to be outcasts for the remainder of their lives.

The cove in Bounty Bay as it appeared when the mutineers landed in January 1790. The painting, prepared for the book describing the visit in 1825 of HMS Blossom, under the command of Captain Beechey, provides a vivid impression of the difficulty of landing in the surf and the danger posed by rocks. The situation remained unchanged until 1886, when the crew of HMS Pelican blew away several rocks, using explosives, a process which continues to present times.

15

This picture of part of a model, made by the author, depicts some of the frantic activity at the Landing Place on Pitcairn Island while the mutineers were emptying and dismantling the *Bounty* before setting the ship on fire. In the boat can be seen an anvil and a vice used on the island for over 100 years. At the bow, John Mills, gunner's mate, removes a cannon ball, and holding a bucket is William McCoy, able seaman, who later used it to distil an intoxicating liquor with tragic consequences. Most remarkable of all is the earthenware jar on the shoulder of a Polynesian girl. This jar was still being used to carry water in the 1930s.

One

In the Beginning

Pitcairn Island seemed to be the ideal refuge for the mutineers, but two main factors prevented it from being a happy place. Firstly, the Polynesian men were not given any land and were treated as slaves, and secondly, the shortage of women meant that six of the natives had to share three wives. This delicate situation worsened when the wife of John Williams fell to her death from a cliff while gathering bird's eggs. To make good his loss he took one of the natives' wives. This meant that the six natives had to share two women, a situation which led to one dreadful day in 1793 when the resentful natives murdered five of the mutineers, probably including Fletcher Christian. Shortly afterwards they themselves were slain, mostly by the Polynesian women who had formed attachments with the mutineers.

Of the four remaining mutineers, McCoy became intoxicated after distilling a whisky-like spirit from the ti plant and committed suicide by jumping into the sea. Quintal too got drunk and threatened to kill Young and Adams (then known as Smith). They got in first and beheaded him with an axe.

Midshipman Edward Young died from natural causes in 1800, leaving John Adams as the sole surviving male along with an estimated ten women and twenty-three children.

Before he died, Young improved Adams' writing and reading abilities using a bible brought ashore from the *Bounty*. Realizing that drastic changes were necessary, Adams used religious tracts to introduce law and order, thereby creating a peaceful society which became unique in the Pacific, the basic tenets of which survive today.

Fletcher Christian in his 'cave', as shown in a book printed in 1895. The cave is incorrectly depicted in a sea-cliff face. The cave was difficult to get into, easy to defend and gave a good view of the sea. The leader of the mutiny is said to have spent many lonely hours there looking seawards, fearful that a searching ship of the British Navy would find the tiny island.

Christian's Cave today. In the early days it was screened by trees and not so readily visible.

Question.—Christian you say was shot?

Answer.—Yes he was.

Q.—By whom?

A.—A black fellow shot him.

Q.—What cause do you assign for the murder?

A.—I know no reason, except a jealousy which I have heard then existed between the people of Otaheite and the English—Christian was shot in the back while at work in his yam plantation.

Q.—What became of the man who killed him?

A.—Oh! that black fellow was shot afterwards by an Englishman.

Q.—Was there any other disturbance between the Otaheiteans and English, after the death of Christian?

A.—Yes, the black fellows rose, shot two Englishmen, and wounded John Adams, who is now the only remaining man who came in the Bounty.

Q.—How did Adams escape being murdered?

A.—He hid himself in the wood, and the same night, the women enraged at the murder of the English, to whom they were more partial than their countrymen, rose and put every Otaheitean to death in their sleep. This saved Adams, his wounds were soon healed, and although old, he now enjoys good health.

This account of the death of Fletcher Christian is given in a book describing the visit of HMS *Briton* to Pitcairn Island in 1814. The *Briton* was the first British ship to visit the island after the discovery of the mutineers' hideout in 1808 by Captain Folger in the American whaler *Topaz*. Later, different accounts of the event were given by John Adams. Another early account states that John Adams himself accidentally shot Christian in 1800 to prevent him leaving the island on a passing ship. Yet another story is that Christian did indeed manage to return to England and lived with friends in Westmorland. Weight to this unlikely story was given by Captain Heywood who, while walking along Fore Street, Plymouth Dock, found himself behind a man whose shape looked like that of Christian. Heywood quickened his pace, whereupon the stranger turned. He looked like Christian, but ran off into the crowd.

A romantic portrayal of Fletcher Christian and his Tahitian consort Mauatea, whom he later renamed Isabella. The picture is signed by Brenda Christian, a fifth-generation direct descendent of the mutineer.

William Christian, born in 1960, cultivating the plot of land on which Fletcher Christian is believed to have been killed in 1793. However, would anyone dare to disturb the possible grave of his ancestor?

This illustration in a one hundred year-old book is entitled 'Old John Adams teaches the children'.

The rugged, rock-bound, wave-lashed shoreline of Pitcairn Island is evident in this view. Landings of major stores were, and still are, only possible in Bounty Bay, and require great skill.

An early church and school house.

Ancient Polynesian markings at the foot of the steep cliff on the south coast known as The Rope. With imagination many meanings can be given to the drawings, but it is not known what they really portray.

John Adams, drawn a few years before his death in 1829. As the last surviving mutineer he organized the ten women and twenty-three children left after the massacres into a model society. A book published in 1896 contained the following comment 'Of all the repentant criminals on record, the most interesting, perhaps, is John Adams. Nor do we know where to find a more beautiful example of the value of early instruction than in the history of this man, who, having run a full career of most kinds of vice, was checked by an interval of leisure and reflection and a sense of new duties awakened by the power of natural affection'.

Before the well-educated Edward Young died in December 1800, he used the *Bounty*'s bible and prayer book to help Adams improve his reading and writing abilities. One result was this prayer written by John Adams and used by him on Sundays.

> for the Lord's Day Morning
> Suffer me not o Lord to waste
> this Day in Sin or folly
> But Let me worship thee with
> much Delight teach me to know
> more of thee and to Serve thee Better
> than ever I have Done Before,
> that I may Be fitter to Dwell
> in heaven, where thy worship and
> Service are everlasting, Amen
>
> John Adams

John Adams' house, built by himself on the level ground at the top of the Hill of Difficulty. Some timber taken from the top of the *Bounty* was probably used in its construction.

John Adams' grave in the nineteenth century. The original headstone consisted of wood covered with copper sheeting from the *Bounty*. It is the only grave that survives today of a mutineer.

An early two-storey house, drawn during the visit by Captain Beechey in HMS *Blossom* in 1825. Christian's Cave is visible in the middle background.

In the 1930s this was the oldest house on Pitcairn. Many of the early houses used timber taken from the *Bounty* before the ship was burnt. By a strange quirk of fate, while Pitcairn was empty after the inhabitants were moved to Norfolk Island in the 1850s, the shipwrecked crew of the *Wild Wave* reached the island and used wood from the houses to help make a boat to reach an inhabited island.

To take missionaries to the island the Adventist Church in America ordered a special schooner in 1890 which was named *Pitcairn*. This completed the first of six visits on 25 November 1890. Following a mass baptism in a rock pool eighty-two islanders were accepted into Adventism. The church encouraged a good and friendly way of life of which the basic aspects are still evident.

An early thatched roof mission house, illustrated in Rosalind Young's book on Pitcairn.

A house on Pitcairn, 1898.

Another house on Pitcairn. The glass windows are noteworthy.

Enlarged Parliament House and church, sketched in 1898.

A view of Bounty Bay from the top of the cliff in the late nineteenth century. Little had been done to clear any rocks dotting the entrance to the landing area. Sheds, however, had been built to house the longboats and fishing canoes.

An early view of the Landing Place captioned 'The Beach'. Note that logs have been laid to form a slipway, easing the laborious tasks of launching and beaching longboats.

An early lighthouse lit by an oil lamp. Located on top of the cliff facing Bounty Bay, the light was used by islanders to help guide them home to the tiny landing area.

Children collecting firewood in one of the unusual island wheelbarrows developed to suit the steep and slippery pathways. Curved ends to the handles and side skids helped when going down steep paths and the shape of the side pieces prevented the barrows tipping over sideways.

Apart from the planks salvaged from the *Bounty*, all timber had to be handsawn. Here islanders are making planks at the island saw pit. It was hard work, particularly for the lower man, who was responsible for the strenuous, downward cutting stroke.

Children playing with smaller versions of the island's wheelbarrows, that for many years were the major means of moving goods.

An islander's house in the late nineteenth century. The thatch used for roofing was in later years changed to sheets of corrugated iron, as this could be readily used to collect rainwater. Note the neat fence around the front of the house.

Seventh-Day Adventist Church. Building began in 1900 and was completed in 1907. The church was used for nearly fifty years, until it was demolished in September 1944. A new church was dedicated on 11 November 1944.

A Pitcairn wheelbarrow being manhandled up the Hill of Difficulty with an important load – a barrel of fuel oil. A second barrel is being rolled up the hill.

A Pitcairn wheelbarrow with another important load – the school teacher's son.

Pitcairn Island school in the early twentieth century. Teachers came from the church until the mid-1950s, when the government assumed the administration of the school. A policy adopted then, and still in operation today, is for an Education Officer to be appointed every two years by the Governor of Pitcairn, in Auckland, New Zealand. Pitcairn was the first British community to introduce compulsory education for children.

The home of Edgar R. Christian, early unofficial postmaster and magistrate.

A primitive early arrowroot mill, used to mill flour.

The home of Pastor David Nield, who married Rosalind Young, a descendent of the mutineer Edward Young and a well-known native island author.

The Landing Place in the mid-1950s. Numerous thatched buildings house the longboats and fishing canoes.

An early Court House.

To help get supplies up to Adamstown from the Landing Place, a platform known as the 'Flying Fox' was used. Supported on a cable, the platform was hauled up and down.

A load of Christmas presents donated by the Santa Claus Club of the South Pacific, being hoisted up on the 'Flying Fox'.

Two islanders paddle their way out of the landing cove to catch fish. The waves breaking on the far shore give some idea of the danger of the task.

A longboat braves heavy surf to reach the open sea.

PITCAIRN - ISLAND.   A 7300.

An early photograph of Pitcairn Island.

A view of Pitcairn Island as seen from a passing liner in the 1930s.

Two

Relics from the Bounty

A surprising number of items of equipment carried on the *Bounty* have survived. The most significant relic is the K2 chronometer, which was used by John Adams to prove that the *Bounty* had indeed been to Pitcairn when the island was 'found' by Captain Folger in the *Topaz* in 1808. The chronometer is now preserved in the National Maritime Museum at Greenwich in London. However, the most precious relic as far the Pitcairn Islanders are concerned is the *Bounty* Bible brought ashore from the ship and now kept on the island.

The only piece of the *Bounty* itself which has survived to the present day, apart from some rotting timber frames, copper sheathing and nails encrusted in rocks at the bottom of Bounty Bay, is a piece of the rudder. This was found by Parkin Christian in the mid-1930s. When salvaged the remnant was over 13ft long, but during the following years pieces were purloined for sale or cut off at the request of visitors. It remained on Pitcairn until 1944 when it was transferred to Fiji for safe keeping, along with a hull nail and a piece of the lead sheeting used to floor the great cabin where the breadfruit was stored. Fiji is an appropriate place for a relic of the *Bounty*, as Captain Bligh was one of the first explorers to chart the area around the island as he sailed through.

In 1843 a salvaged *Bounty* cannon fired while being loaded, killing the island magistrate and injuring two others. A further two cannons were raised in 1973, one of which is on display on Pitcairn. The fourth and last cannon was raised in January 1999. After undergoing preservation treatment in Australia, it will be returned to Pitcairn.

Many small artefacts such as bottles, Fletcher Christian's sword and Fryer's telescope are in private hands. One of the most curious relics is John Adam's sailor's pigtail, which was taken to England in 1853.

The original John Adams grave marker. It consisted of two pieces of *Bounty* timber covered in copper sheeting from the hull. The inscription, made of a nail-pricked holes, reads: 'Sacred to the memory of John Adams who died March 1829, aged 65 years'. The relic is now in the possession of the National Maritime Museum at Greenwich, London.

Part of what was thought to be the *Bounty* rudder being proudly displayed after its recovery from Bounty Bay in the 1930s.

Two precious artefacts taken off the *Bounty* by the mutineers were the anvil (right) and the vice, seen here being used in the 1930s by Benjamin Young. These two historic tools were in daily use for 150 years before they were replaced by newer items.

The *Bounty* inventory listed fourteen dozen axes of various sizes, for trading with the Tahitians. This particular axe head hangs in the office of the Secretary, Pitcairn Island.

A PIECE OF HISTORY RETURNS TO ENGLAND

H.M. Armed Vessel "BOUNTY" was dismantled, scuttled, and burned off PITCAIRN ISLAND, 1790.

A chip from the Bounty's rudder.

Verified by:-
Bert Christian, Asst. Govt. Secretary,

Roy P. Clark, Postmaster.

Roy P. Clark, P.M.
Pitcairn Island
South Pacific Ocean

PITCAIRN ISLANDS
2d

MAY 12 57

Appropriately titled 'A piece of history' this tiny piece of wood is from the rudder of the *Bounty*. The postcard, with a picture of the oldest house on Pitcairn, is dated May 1957. It was verified by Bert Christian and Roy Clark, Pitcairn's Postmaster for many years.

A most remarkable relic of the *Bounty* is this earthenware jar that was still being used to carry water in the 1930s, as shown by this photograph taken at that time.

Bernice Christian, in her cosy front room, with the jar from the *Bounty*. The jar is now in the hands of relatives on Norfolk Island, but it is hoped that its final resting place will be the museum on Pitcairn Island. Bernice died in 1994, aged ninety-five.

An artist's colour box thought to have been taken from the *Bounty*. As the only artist on the vessel was Captain Bligh, who was a talented watercolourist, the box may have belonged to him personally.

The only piece of the *Bounty* hull that survives today is the section of the rudder, located by Parkin Christian in 1935. The 13ft remnant, including three hinge gudgeons, was salvaged from the wreck site. Over the following years pieces were cut off and sold as souvenirs.

In 1944 the British Admiralty decided that the rudder relic, by then $6\frac{1}{2}$ft long, should be sent to Fiji for safe keeping. It is now displayed in front of a large copy of the well-known picture of the mutiny painted by Robert Dodd in 1790.

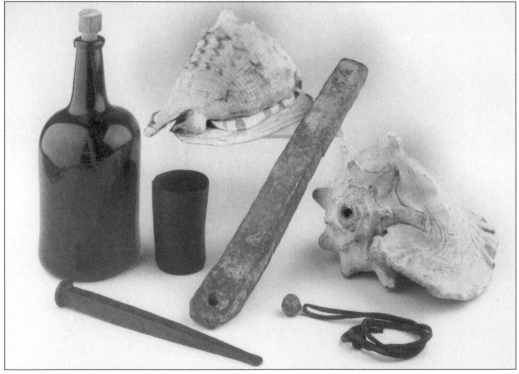

The lid of this snuff box is engraved 'The copper of which this box consists was taken from the Bounty sloop of war that was lost on Pitcairn Island South Seas'.

Items from the *Bounty*, including a sounding lead, copper nail and a bottle. The horn mug and bullet-weight are said by descendants of Bligh to have been used during his epic open boat voyage to East Timor.

K2, the chronometer used on the *Bounty* and taken to Pitcairn Island. It was given to Captain Folger, of the American ship *Topaz*, in 1808 as proof of the whereabouts of the lost *Bounty*. After a variety of other owners, some of dubious character, it was given to the National Maritime Museum, Greenwich, where, after meticulous restoration, it still ticks away the time.

A copper kettle used by the mutineer McCoy to distil a potent alcohol from the roots of the ti plant, with disastrous results. During one fit of drunkenness he fastened a stone around his neck, threw himself off the rocks into the sea and was drowned. The kettle, with much of the rim cut away, is now preserved on Norfolk Island.

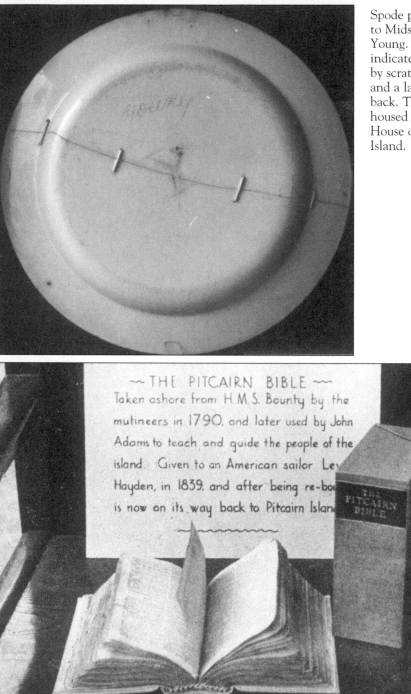

Spode plate belonging to Midshipman Edward Young. The mutineer indicated his ownership by scratching his name and a large Y on the back. The plate is now housed in Government House on Norfolk Island.

~THE PITCAIRN BIBLE~
Taken ashore from H.M.S. Bounty by the mutineers in 1790, and later used by John Adams to teach and guide the people of the island. Given to an American sailor Le\ Hayden, in 1839, and after being re-bo\ is now on its way back to Pitcairn Islan\

Two priceless bibles from the *Bounty* still exist after 200 years. One, the 'Christian Bible', belonged to Fletcher Christian, and is now kept in the New York Public Library. The second, the 'Bounty Bible', was the official ship's bible. Rebound with a prayer book, it is now Pitcairn's most precious relic of the mutiny. It is kept in a special glass-topped case in the Seventh-Day Adventist church in Adamstown.

The bow anchor from the Bounty was found by the crew of the yacht *Yankee* in 1957 and brought ashore. The 12ft relic was distinguished by its straight V-flukes, as rounded flukes did not come into use until about 1810.

The anchor is now displayed on a concrete plinth in the square in the centre of Adamstown. It is shown here with Fred Christian (left) and Parkin Christian, both great, great grandsons of Fletcher Christian.

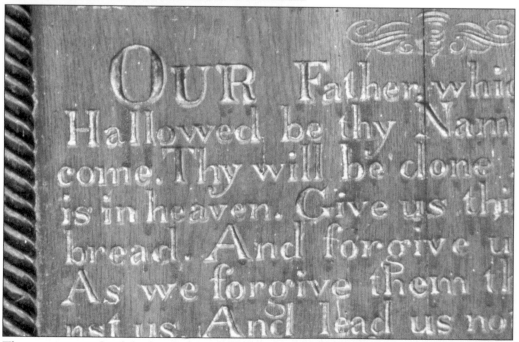

A medical book, titled *Domestic Medicine* belonged to the *Bounty* surgeon Thomas Huggan, who died of alcoholism on Tahiti. The book went with the *Bounty* to Pitcairn, where it was used by the islanders until 1837. The book is now preserved in the National Maritime Museum, Greenwich.

The opening words of the Lord's Prayer, thought to have been painstakingly carved by John Adams into wood taken from the *Bounty*. Another panel contains the Ten Commandments. The two panels were taken to Norfolk Island in the exodus in 1856. Sadly this panel was destroyed by fire, but a replacement has been carved.

A prayer book from the *Bounty*, alongside the original Pitcairn Island Register Book. This is a remarkable record of births and deaths on the island and of ships visiting Pitcairn from 1790 until 1853. The first entry in the register reads '1790 January 23rd H M Ship *Bounty* burned at Pitcairn Island. Same year died Fasto, wife of John Williams'.

Possibly the last major relic of the *Bounty* to be found is this deck cannon, shown as it was recovered in January 1999. One of four carried, it is currently undergoing preservation in Australia, after which it will be displayed in the Pitcairn Island Museum.

The barrel of one of the four deck cannons carried on the Bounty. It was taken from Pitcairn to Norfolk Island in the 1856 migration.

Over the years the condition of the cannon deteriorated. It was refurbished in 1971 and is now displayed in Givernment House on Norfolk Island.

Three

Migration to Norfolk Island

By 1850 the population of Pitcairn had grown to 156 and was still increasing. The cultivatable land could not support this number and the fish had deserted the coastal waters. The need to find a new home was obvious.

A previous move to Tahiti in 1831 had proved disastrous, with fifteen islanders succumbing to diseases against which they had no immunity. Because of this experience the islanders insisted that they should be moved to an uninhabited island. It was decided that the best place available was Norfolk Island, 3,700 miles to the west. This was bigger than Pitcairn and the now departed convicts had left much cultivated land, roads and houses.

To help the move the government of Queen Victoria in England provided the ship HMS *Morayshire*. So, on 3 May 1856, the entire population of Pitcairn, numbering 193 persons, left on the ship. After a harrowing voyage Norfolk Island was reached and 194 passengers disembarked, baby Reuben Denison Christian having been born during the journey.

However, in spite of the advantages of Norfolk Island, the Pitcairners found it difficult to settle in the sturdy stone buildings built when it was a penal colony. Within two years many grew homesick and in January 1859 a group of sixteen, mostly members of the Young family, left Norfolk to return 'home'. Had the party not arrived when it did, the story of Pitcairn could have ended, or taken a markedly different course. For, soon after they arrived, a French man-of-war anchored offshore, with the intention of claiming the vacant island on behalf of the French government!

In 1863 the small community was given a boost with the return of more Pitcairners, including Thursday October Christian's family of twelve.

For the first time the original settlers of Pitcairn became divided, and have since evolved as two individual communities separated by a vast stretch of ocean, but linked by a common history and ancestors.

HMS *Morayshire*, the ship provided by the British Government to move the Pitcairn Islanders to Norfolk Island, nearly 4,000 miles away.

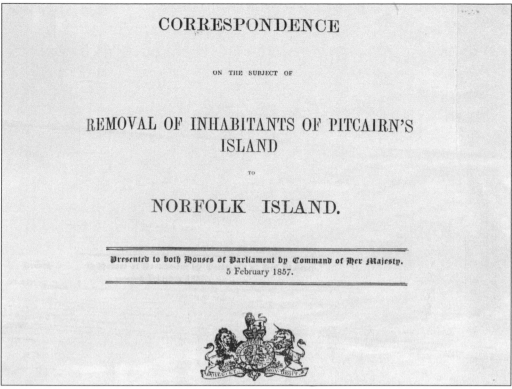

CORRESPONDENCE

ON THE SUBJECT OF

REMOVAL OF INHABITANTS OF PITCAIRN'S ISLAND

TO

NORFOLK ISLAND.

Presented to both Houses of Parliament by Command of Her Majesty.
5 February 1857.

British governmental pages relating to the move to Norfolk Island are preserved in the House of Lords, London.

The Pitcairners
OF NORFOLK ISLAND

Rosalind Amelia Young
AUTHORESS AND HISTORIAN

27c
Norfolk Island

"Rosalind Amelia Young"
1853 - 1924

In 1856 as a three year old child with other descendants of the Pitcairners, Rosalind travelled from Pitcairn Island to Norfolk Island in the ship "Morayshire". Rosalind spent her childhood on Norfolk Island before returning to Pitcairn Island with her parents. On Pitcairn she documented most of the events of the Mutiny of the Bounty and the story of the Pitcairn Islanders. Authoritatively the recording of the Descendants and her notes on Norfolk Island have been invaluable in tracing the full history.

First published in 1894 her book had eight printings up until 1924. In 1907 she married Pastor David Nield.

Rosalind Amelia Young was one of the youngest Pitcairners to go to Norfolk Island. Later she returned to Pitcairn, where she wrote a historically valuable account of the early days on the island.

A postage stamp issued in 1981 shows the last family to leave Pitcairn struggling down the Hill of Difficulty to Bounty Bay, where the *Morayshire* is anchored offshore.

A farewell view of Pitcairn as the *Morayshire* leaves for the long and harrowing voyage to Norfolk Island.

The family, previously depicted leaving Pitcairn, disembarking at Kingston Jetty, Norfolk Island, along with other islanders.

Two newcomers survey their new homeland from a hill overlooking the landing area.

Norfolk Island Historic Cemetery, the resting place for so many of the descendants of the mutiny on the *Bounty*. The tombstones in the foreground are from the convict penal colony era. Those in the background commemorate descendants of the mutineers.

Not the tombstone of the leader of the mutiny on the *Bounty*, but that of Fletcher Christian Nobbs, who was born on Pitcairn in 1833. He married Susan Quintal, also born on Pitcairn, in 1833.

Headstone of Arthur Quintal, son of the mutineer Matthew Quintal. He was born on Pitcairn Island in 1794 and he died on Norfolk Island on 1873.

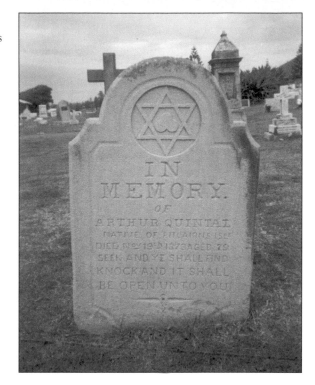

Tombstone of Mary, the only daughter of Fletcher Christian and Isabella. Born on Pitcairn Island in 1793, she died on Norfolk Island in 1866, aged seventy-three, not sixty-nine, as engraved.

The blacksmith's forge, built at the time of the Pitcairn migration to Norfolk Island in the mid-1850s. Like most forges, it has no windows, so that the blacksmith can more accurately estimate the temperature of heated iron by its colour.

Norfolk Island Pitcairn descendants. Back row, left to right: Diana Adams (née McCoy) 1838-1929, her husband Josiah Chester Adams 1830-1907, Susan Nobbs (née Quintal) 1833-1917. Front row; John Forrester Young 1852-1913, Eliza Loisa (Lil) Young (née Nobbs) 1856-1920, Arthur Quintal 1816-1902 (son of Arthur and Catherine Quintal (née McCoy).

Pauline (Polly) Adams, the first of eleven children of John Adams, grandson of the mutineer, born in May 1844 on Pitcairn. Polly died on Norfolk Island at the age of seventy-six in May 1920.

The author with one of two panels believed to have been carved by the mutineer John Adams on wood salvaged from the *Bounty*. The two panels were taken to Norfolk Island in 1856. The second panel, including the last six commandments and the Lord's Prayer, was destroyed by fire, but a replacement has now been carved.

Memories of Pitcairn abound on Norfolk Island. This sign shows the way to a tour of unusual buildings relating to the early days of the Pitcairn islanders' settlement.

The name of the leader of the mutiny on the *Bounty* has been adopted by one of the fine hotels on Norfolk Island. Many roads and shops are named after other mutineers.

The Bounty Folk Museum on Norfolk Island. This is full of island history and contains an extensive collection of magazines and documents relating to Pitcairn.

Exhibits in the museum include an original copy of the book written by Bligh describing the voyage of the *Bounty* to Tahiti to collect breadfruit, and a model of the open boat in which he made his epic 3,600 mile journey to Timor. Nearby is a full-size display showing Bligh in his cabin at the moment the mutineers took control of the *Bounty*.

HMS *Pelican* under full sail. Sloops of the Osprey class had a composite hull of steel and wood. Designed to combine handiness with speed, the ship could travel using its sails, or with its steam- powered screw.

Four

Visit to Pitcairn

While on patrol in the Pacific in the 1880s, the British Navy sloop HMS *Pelican* visited Pitcairn Island. The visit was recorded in the personal log of a member of the crew named Stephen Gundy. Extracts from this log give a fascinating insight into life on the island in those days:

'On getting through the surf we had a steep hill to climb before we got to the houses. This is merely a goat track at the edge of a steep rock. In some places it made me giddy to look down, and my foot slipped several times.

'A Mrs Young kindly volunteered to be the guide of my party. We visited the grave of John Adams, the last survivor of the *Bounty*. This grave does not appear to be kept as it should, just a few stones placed around it and with a wild geranium planted at the head.

'We paid a visit to Mrs McCoy's house where her daughter played us several Hymns, we joining in and making the house shake. The house was very clean, and one thing put me in mind of dear old England was a canary in a cage over one of the bunks.

'I noticed in several of the houses pictures of the Royal Family, not framed but nailed up on the wall so that a stranger on entering could see it at once. The girls are very simple, and if you only speak to them they laugh and take what you say, if ever so simple, as a great joke. By books I have read the girls are supposed to be very moral and religious, but I cannot but take the word of mouth from Miss A. Young, also Mrs McCoy, both who said the people on the island are not so good as the outside world would make them to be.

'As we steamed slowly away, the two boats pulled up alongside when the men, joining in with the ladies, sang three verses of *God Save Our Queen*, then standing up in their boats they gave us three hearty cheers. At the finish our Drum and Pipe band on the poop played *God Save Our Queen* and *Old Lang Syne*'.

HMS *Pelican*, a sloop of the British Navy's Osprey class of warships in the nineteenth century.

> Catherine Edith Warren,
> gave tracts and Valentine Oct: 19. 1886
>
> C. E. Warren was also on board with Miss Young she is the daughter of a shipwrecked sailor!

Several islanders signed Stephen Gundy's personal log during the visit of HMS *Pelican*, including Catherine Edith Warren. Stephen Gundy added the explanatory comment.

HMS *Pelican* at anchor, with its deck shielded from the tropical sun.

Impression of Pitcairn Island, prepared a few years before the visit of HMS *Pelican*.

A rare signature of Thursday October Christian, the grandson of Fletcher Christian, obtained during the visit of the HMS *Pelican*.

Thursday October Christian in front of his thatched house.

Full names of some of my shipmates who sailed in the
Pelican, with their ratings. and some of the Pitcairns.

Henry Rooke. W. R. Mess 11 an
Alfred Robert Stephenson 3 Mᵗ Mate
John I. Tay.   a gentleman taking passage for
James. Benjamin. Colmer. Stone. Ship 1ˢᵗ Assistant purser
Y. W Hillman Captain Hoald
J. Ginnis Armourer
William Alfred. Young. Pitcairns Islan.
                    23 yrs   October 18 1855
Ernest. Heywood Christian Pitcairns Island.
                    23 yrs   October, 18, 1886,
James Burl Christian
                        October. 13. 1886
Samuel. Henry. Salmon. Young. Pitcairn Island. Cousin
                        October. 18. 96.
Benjamin Stanley Young. Pitcairn's Island,
                    24 yrs October 18. 1896
Leonard. Elliott. Dashwood. Christian
                    Pitcairn Island
                        October 18, 1886
William Henry Childers Young
                    Pitcairn Island
                        October. 18. 18-86
James Russell Mc Coy. Octᵉ 18ᵗʰ 1886.

A remarkable page in the *Pelican* Personal Log bearing signatures of three members of the Christian family and four Youngs. Also of historic interest is the signature of John Tay, who left the *Pelican* to remain on the island. A missionary of the Seventh-Day Adventist Church, he played a significant part in converting the Pitcairners to this branch of Christianity.

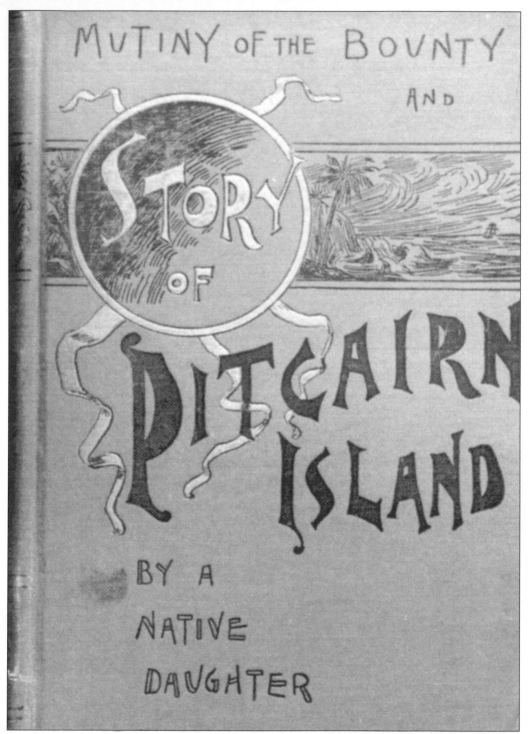

The cover of Rosalind Amelia Young's book *Mutiny on the Bounty and the Story of Pitcairn Island*. First published in 1894, copies are now rare. It provides a valuable account of the early days on the island and the likely fate of the mutineers.

Rosalind Amelia Young

Pitcairn Island

October 19th 1886

R. Amelia Young descendant from Midshipman Young of H. M. S. Bounty - schoolmistress, wrote her name here on board H. M. S. "Pelican" on the evening of 19th October 1886 at Pitcairn Island, she was the last lady on board;

Rosalind Young's signature in the *Pelican* Personal Log, with an explanatory comment added by Stephen Gundy. She was the teacher at the island school for several years.

The grave of Rosalind Young is one of the few marked sites on Pitcairn Island.

John Tay, the missionary from the Seventh-Day Adventist church who settled on the island.

P/10G

Pitcairn 19. Octr. 86.

To Mrs Young

Chocolate 15. lbs.
Tea 1. lb.
Thread 1. pcket.
Knives 1. No.
Combs 2. No.
Drill 6. Yards
Scisors 1. No.
Buttons 1. Packet.

To Christian 2 lbs. Tea 5. lbs. Sugar Candles

An entry in the personal log recording provisions supplied to Mrs Young and Christian.

YEAR	NUMBER OF MILES			TOTAL	NUMBER OF DAYS			TOTAL
	Under Steam	Under Sail	Under Steam & Sail	MILES	Under Steam	Under Sail	Under Steam & Sail	DAYS
1884	2618.1	8123.1	2914.5	13655.7	19(days) 15 ¼ (hrs)	63 1¾	21 12¾	104 5¾
1885	8846.0	1148.0	8034.1	18028.1	60 8½	10 1½	45 2¼	115 12
1886	2290.4	9161.0	1661.1	13112.5	15 8½	75 1¼	12 1½	102 11
1887	5826.3	1402.4	1381.9	8610.6	40 23¼	15 11½	9 14¼	66 1
Totals	19,580.8	19,834.5	13,991.6	53,406.9	136 7½	163 16	88 6¾	388 6¼

An unusual table in the personal log recording the distances covered and the days using sail and steam power.

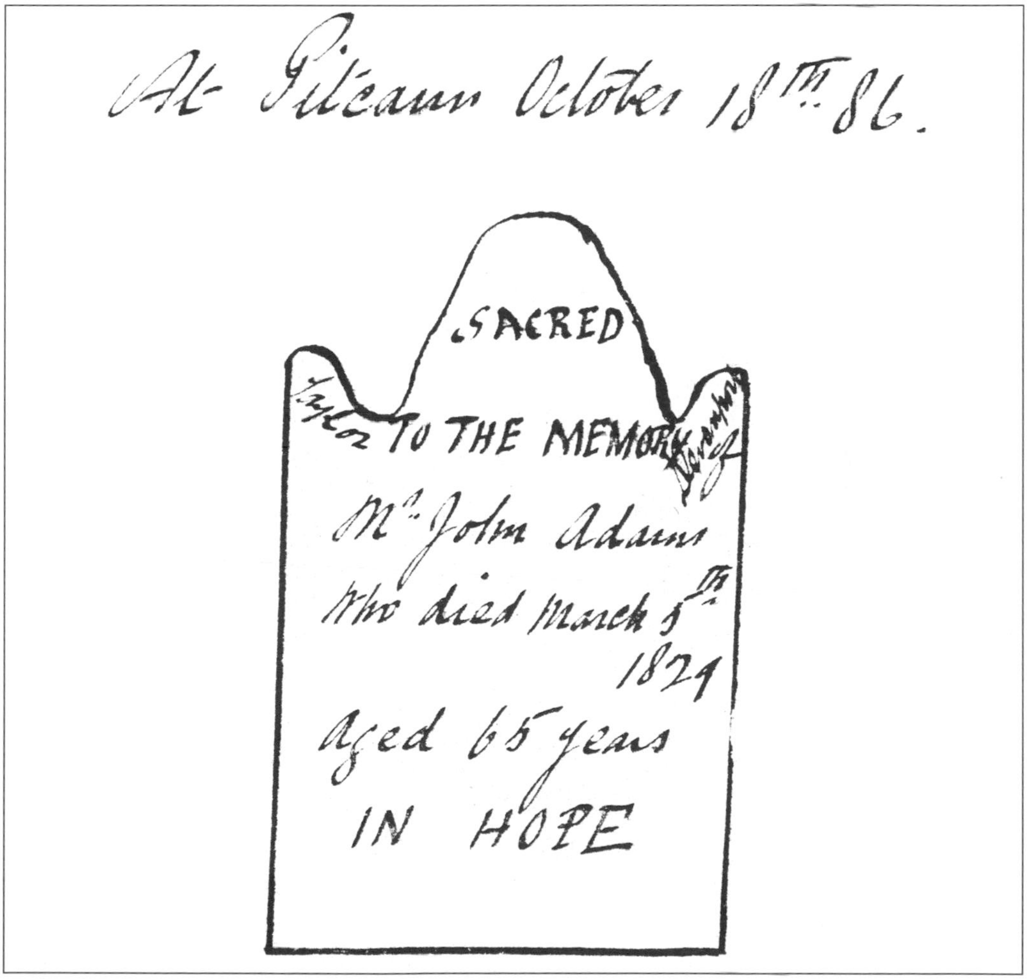

A sketch of Adam's gravestone, drawn anonymously in the personal log, is evidence of the respect in which he was held and his lasting influence. John Adams was the last of the mutineers who, after years of tragedy and murder, led the islanders to a model way of life.

The rugged, surf-pounded coastline of Pitcairn has no easy access from the sea. A concrete quay in Bounty Bay is the only place for a reasonably safe landing. Landings can also be made at Tedside, and canoes can be launched at several places.

Five

Pitcairn Longboats

'First we crunched into rocks to the starboard side of the bay. Then with a thud we hit the large rocks on the port side, and then two huge waves completely swamped the boat. The second boat had an even worse time. It smashed against the cliff face, then spun around like a top. Some of the men tried to jump ashore with precious articles of cargo, only to be swept off their feet. The sea's final effort was to carry the heavily laden boat sideways up the steep slide, with men fleeing before it. One man tripped and fell, but was saved when the boat smashed into the stern of a housed boat, drove farther into the boat shed, and finally stopped.'

This was how one passenger described his landing on Pitcairn Island as he came ashore from the 20,000-ton liner *Ruahine* in 1957.

The longboats are the lifeline of Pitcairn Island. All supplies of food, equipment (with one notable exception, the Island's bulldozer, which was air dropped by the Royal New Zealand Air Force in 1983) and material, and all people, have to be transferred from passing ships to a longboat in which they are ferried ashore.

For 150 years the whaleboats, as they were known, were made on the island. The boats were 38ft long, and were manned by up to fourteen oarsmen, a coxswain and a lookout at the stern who, then as now, has the job of looking for a good wave to get them through the pounding surf.

Today, the wooden man-powered longboats of yesteryear have been replaced by modern, engine-powered, aluminium boats, specially designed for their unique task. The use of such boats naturally eases the transfer of supplies and people, but in anything but the calmest of weathers great skill is still required when landing and leaving.

A longboat approaching a visiting ship.

Longboats are the lifeline of Pitcairn Island. All people, food, fuel, stores and goods have to be ferried ashore in the boats.

Up until the early 1980s the 38ft longboats were built on the island. Here work has started on the keel of a new boat. When complete they were manhandled down the Hill of Difficulty to the Landing Place.

Islanders board a longboat to barter souvenirs with a passing ship.

'Headman greeting the Captain' was the original caption of this early picture of a longboat full of islanders and souvenirs approaching a visiting liner.

A longboat returning to the Landing Place in heavy seas. Note the lookout standing in the stern who watches for a 'safe' wave before entering the bay.

Boat sheds in the 1930s. Note the wooden slipway of the type used by early islanders. The thatched roofs of the sheds were replaced with corrugated iron sheets in the 1960s.

A longboat returns to the Landing Place after visiting a passing ship. The rowing skills of the islanders were renowned throughout the Pacific.

Islanders, with their carvings and other articles for sale, clamber up the side of a visiting liner.

An islander climbs up the side of the SS *Ionic* in a heavy sea in 1921.

Building a longboat. The ribs were usually made of locally hewn timber, but the planks were imported. The design follows that of a boat given to the island by Queen Victoria.

A longboat about to leave the Landing Place. Twelve men were needed to row the big boats safely.

Two longboats full of islanders come alongside the RMS *Remuera* in 1916.

Two diesel-powered launches and two manned rowing boats prepare to go to a ship to bring back a large quantity of stores.

This picture on the front cover of a Swedish magazine in the 1930s gives a good indication of the sturdy construction of a Pitcairn-built longboat.

A newly-built boat being manhandled down the Hill of Difficulty.

An island-built longboat of the mid-1950s. The boats were 38ft long and could carry five tons of cargo.

The new landing stage, built in the 1980s, significantly eases the landing and unloading of supplies and people.

Two modern aluminium longboats, known as *Tub* and *Moss*, in the boatshed at the Landing Place. The two boats go out together whenever possible, to provide a measure of safety should one founder.

This unusual view emphasizes the very small size of the Landing Place in Bounty Bay and the steepness of the adjacent cliffs. The Hill of Difficulty is left of centre.

Six

People and Places

For a tiny island, with a small population, Pitcairn has a remarkable abundance of interesting people and places.

The people are descended from the mutineers of the *Bounty* who landed on the island in 1790, with six Polynesian men, twelve Polynesian women and a baby girl.

Since the early days outsiders have settled and married into the founding families. Sometimes communities that are so closely related experience deterioration in mental and physical abilities, but there is no evidence of this on Pitcairn Island. There are a great variety of features among the islanders, so it is difficult to describe a typical Pitcairner. Most, however, have weather-worn features and all have brown eyes. Only two of the original mutineer families survive today, the Christians and the Youngs.

The island appears to be the top of a volcano, the base of which is far below the sea. It is rugged and cliff-lined all the way round, nowhere giving easy access from the sea. Only two places, Bounty Bay and the Tedside Landing, offer a reasonably safe landing.

The island abounds in names that link it to its historic past. These either recall a person, such as 'Adam's Rock', 'Jenny's Bread' and 'Brown's Water', or an incident such as 'Where Freddie Fell', 'Nellie Fall' and 'McCoy's Drop'. There are many 'falls'.

All the original mutineers have places named after them, the most famous being 'Christian's Cave' overlooking Adamstown. Until recently one notable name, Quintal, was missing. This has now been rectified by the discovery of a cavern, etched away by the seas on a difficult-to-reach part of the shoreline. This is now known as 'Quintal's Cavern'.

Following page: Map showing many features named after islanders.

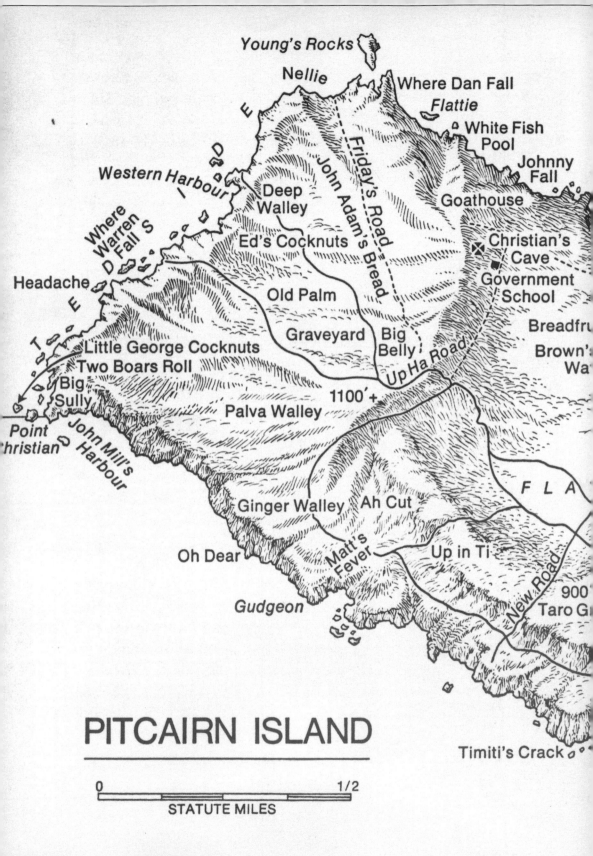

Young's Rocks

Nellie

Where Dan Fall

Flattie

White Fish Pool

Johnny Fall

Western Harbour

Deep Walley

John Adam's Bread

Friday's Road

Goathouse

Ed's Cocknuts

Christian's Cave

Where Warren Fall

Old Palm

Government School

Headache

Graveyard

Big Belly

Breadfru

Brown'

Wa

Little George Cocknuts

Two Boars Roll

Up Ha Road

Big Sully

1100'+

Palva Walley

Point Christian

John Mill's Harbour

Ginger Walley

Ah Cut

F L A

Oh Dear

Matt's Fever

Up in Ti

New Road

Gudgeon

900

Taro G

PITCAIRN ISLAND

Timiti's Crack

0   1/2

STATUTE MILES

am. H. Bryant

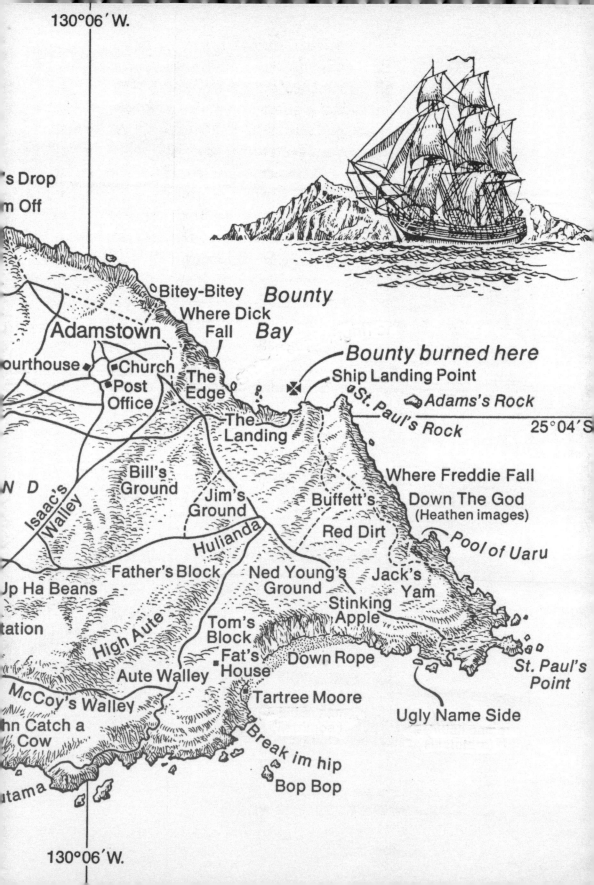

130°06′ W.

's Drop
m Off

Bitey-Bitey   *Bounty*

Where Dick
Fall   *Bay*

Adamstown

ourthouse   Church   *Bounty burned here*
Post   The   Ship Landing Point
Office   Edge   *Adams's Rock*
                                    St. Paul's
                The   Rock
                Landing   25°04′S

                                    Where Freddie Fall
Bill's   Down The God
Ground   Jim's   Buffett's   (Heathen images)
           Ground
N D   Red Dirt   Pool of Uaru
   Isaac's
   Walley   Hulianda
                                              Jack's
           Father's Block   Ned Young's   Yam
Jp Ha Beans   Ground
                                         Stinking
tation   Apple

        High Aute   Tom's
                     Block   Down Rope   St. Paul's
        Aute Walley Fat's   Point
                     House
McCoy's Walley   Ugly Name Side
hn Catch a
   Cow   Tartree Moore
utama   Break im hip
                         Bop Bop

130°06′ W.

Sugar cane grinding. The juice is used to make molasses. A good deal of co-operation is required when it is time to grind the cane.

An islander proudly displays a model of the *Bounty*, which he has studiously carved and polished, for sale to a tourist from a visiting liner.

Islanders attend a special service in the first Seventh-Day Adventist church in 1937 to celebrate the coronation of King George VI.

Rosa, John, Arthur and Sarah Young as portrayed in Rosalind Young's book on Pitcairn Island.

An early group of islanders.

Aunt Ann McCoy (1851-1937). One of six children who returned from Norfolk Island, she was the unmarried sister of James McCoy.

An early group of older islanders.

Edwin Christian (1890-1933) with a
bunch of bananas picked from a tree
on his plot of land.

Teachers and children in front of the school house in 1928.

An early group of islanders who have just returned from a visit to a passing ship, c.1920.

Almost the entire population of the island gathered outside the church for this photograph taken in the mid-1920s.

Four generations of Pitcairner Christians. Starting clockwise with the seated lady in the middle: Lilly Warren (born 1878), Lorene Christian, Wilkes Christian, Marjorie Christian, Parkin Christian, holding baby Ralph Christian. The picture was taken from a book covering Pitcairn through six generations.

Thursday October Christian's old home.

Unusual two-storey Pitcairn house of the 1930s. The size of homes today varies considerably. Some have three bedrooms, some as many as twelve. All are simply furnished and are ideal for the lifestyle of Pitcairners.

A clan of Christians. Left to right: John Christian, Burnett Christian, Cora Christian and her husband Elliot Christian, the island magistrate. All the men are brothers.

The 1930 caption for this photograph was 'A wheelbarrow and bliss'.

PRIS 30 ÖRE

Allers

FAMILJ-JOURNAL • N:R 47 • 17 NOVEMBER 1936

Nytt från Pitcairn!

Läs artikeln i detta nummer!

An unusual Pitcairn picture on the cover of the 1936 Swedish family journal 'Allers'. Although Pitcairn has a subtropical climate, with the average temperatures ranging from 19°C in August to 24°C in February, it was hardly the place for an exotic holiday at that time.

Mr Tupen is one of the oldest inhabitants of Pitcairn Island. He is the sole survivor of five giant tortoises brought from the Galapagos Islands between 1937 and 1951. He normally lives in Tedside, but sometimes ambles into Adamstown, where he can destroy a vegetable plot in no time. However, the tortoise is protected by law and anyone who harms or captures the animal will get sixty days in prison.

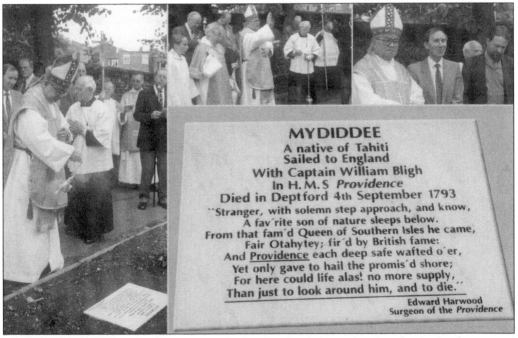

MYDIDDEE
A native of Tahiti
Sailed to England
With Captain William Bligh
In H. M. S *Providence*
Died in Deptford 4th September 1793
"Stranger, with solemn step approach, and know,
A fav'rite son of nature sleeps below.
From that fam'd Queen of Southern Isles he came,
Fair Otahytey; fir'd by British fame:
And Providence each deep safe wafted o'er,
Yet only gave to hail the promis'd shore;
For here could life alas! no more supply,
Than just to look around him, and to die."

Edward Harwood
Surgeon of the *Providence*

Mydiddee was a Tahitian who sailed to England with Bligh on the *Providence* after his second and successful voyage to take breadfruit from Tahiti to the West Indies. Sadly, he fell ill and died soon after arriving in England and was buried at Deptford, London. In 1998 Bishop Jabez Leslie Bryce from Polynesia reconsecrated his grave during a moving ceremony attended by Maurice Bligh, a direct descendant of Captain Bligh. (See top right mini-photograph)

Jerry Miller and Mary Wagonblast getting married on the rocks at Down Issac in October 1984. This is believed to be the first ever wedding of two non-Pitcairners on the island.

Children displaying the Pitcairn Island flag. At the top left is the British Union Flag and the island coat of arms is at the bottom right. Prominent on the shield of the arms are an island wheelbarrow, the Bounty Bible and the *Bounty* anchor.

Saturday service in the Seventh-Day Adventist church built in 1954. The cool interior reflects the tranquillity of the island. General work is forbidden on Saturdays – the Sabbath – but the church allows its members to man the longboats should a ship arrive.

Vernan and Lilian Young, direct descendants of the mutineer Edward Young, with their daughter Margaret, display specimens of island crafts. Items include carvings of birds and fish and a walking stick.

Is this Fletcher Christian? No authentic portrait of him is known to exist. This picture is an enlargement of the portrayal of him standing on the stern of the *Bounty* in the well-known 1790 painting by Robert Dodd, while captain Bligh and eighteen of his loyal crew are being cast adrift. When shown the painting Bligh is reported to have suggested changes to the face so that it represented Christian more accurately.

Using modern police identification techniques, artist Jerry Gordon created this impression of Fletcher Christian. To produce the picture he used portraits of Christian's ancestors, his grandson and photographs of later descendants on Pitcairn. He also took into consideration the description by Captain Bligh who described him as being 'strong, with blackish or very dark brown hair and a dark and very swarthy complexion'. The picture is signed by Steve Christian, a direct descendant of the mutineer.

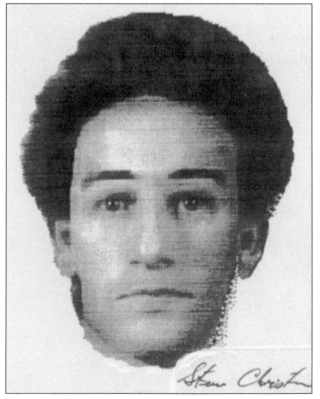

John Adams II, grandson of the mutineer, as depicted on a Norfolk Island stamp. He was born on Pitcairn in 1827 and moved to Norfolk Island during the 1856 exodus. He became a skilled stone cutter and made good dripstones used for filtering water. He died peacefully in 1897.

Wayne Adams is a sixth generation direct descendant of the mutineer. He lives on Norfolk Island where he is known as 'Doggy'. He has the same impressive dark, deep-set eyes shown on portraits of his famous ancestor.

LONDON TO
NEW ZEALAND

via

Panama
Canal

by the

NEW ZEALAND
SHIPPING Cºs

ROYAL MAIL
STEAMERS

SAILINGS FROM PLYMOUTH
EVERY FOUR WEEKS

R.M.S. REMUERA

THE NEW ZEALAND SHIPPING Cº. LTº
INCORPORATED IN NEW ZEALAND

After its discovery by Folger in 1808, Pitcairn's contact with the outside world was by the irregular visits of naval and merchant ships. The opening of the Panama Canal in 1914 increased the visits of ships, as liners of the New Zealand Shipping Company frequently stopped at the island as they travelled from the canal to New Zealand. One regular visitor was the *Remuera*, shown on this leaflet advertising voyages from London to New Zealand and Panama in the 1920s. This passenger service has long been withdrawn and now normally only cargo vessels, on the way from New Zealand and Panama, make regular calls about three or four times a year. In recent years there has been an increase in the number of cruise ships visiting the island. Often these stay for a day, allowing time for passengers to be ferried ashore by longboats.

RMS *Remuera* visiting Pitcairn Island soon after the opening of the Panama Canal. This is the ship shown on the leaflet on the opposite page.

Charles Parkin Christian, chief magistrate on Pitcairn Island in the 1920s, was a direct descendant of the mutineer. Charles was born on the island in November 1885 and died on 15 September 1971.

Bounty Day, Pitcairn. Every year, on 23 January, Pitcairn Islanders celebrate the burning of the *Bounty* in 1790. The morning is spent making a rough model of the ship, using wood, empty drums or an old canoe. This model, made for the celebration in 1957, consisted of a raft of banana trees. It was later filled with twigs and rags, shown loaded in the stern of the towing canoe.

On the shore a large table is erected on the Landing Place. On this is piled fish caught earlier in the day and fried, alongside a mountain of other food. When it gets dark the model ship is towed out into Bounty Bay and set alight, while the islanders tuck into a great meal.

Bounty Day, England. For several years the author in England has duplicated the celebration on Pitcairn. Here a large cardboard and wood model of the Bounty has been boarded by Muffin, the family pet dog, who thinks he is Captain Bligh!

The house is specially decorated for the occasion, even having a wooden bird and other ornaments crafted on Pitcairn. After the burning, guests have breadfruit fritters, made to a Pitcairn recipe, together with dried bananas and dried pineapple specially sent from Pitcairn, as well as plenty of traditional English food.

Reynold Warren, Forester on Pitcairn Island, carrying his share of supplies on Supply Ship Day in October 1984.

Maurice Bligh and Brenda Christian, both descended from the captain and the mutineer, with a model of the Landing Place as it was in 1790. At that time the mutineers were stripping the *Bounty* of timber, fittings and equipment before it was set on fire. Brenda is pointing to a figure representing Fletcher Christian, her great, great, great, great grandfather.

Close up of Mauatua and Fletcher Christian, with the mutineer Issac Martin in the centre. In the background can be seen plates and other items salvaged from the *Bounty*. To the left of Mauatua is a box containing two bibles and the ship's surgeon's medicine book. To the right is a box containing the *Bounty* chronometer, now in the National Maritime Museum in London. The sand, pebbles and rocks used in the model all came from Pitcairn Island.

Jay Warren, island magistrate and environmental officer, poses with his wife Carol and the author in front of William Bligh's house in Lambeth, London, during a visit to England in 1998 to attend a course on horticulture at the Royal Botanic Gardens, Kew.

Jay Warren visits the author's home in Hatfield, north of London, where he had the rare opportunity to see the destination of some of his carvings crafted on Pitcairn Island.

A 'sofa' of Christians. Left to right: Brenda, Mike, Andrew, Joy Allward and Kirsty rest during a visit to the author's home.

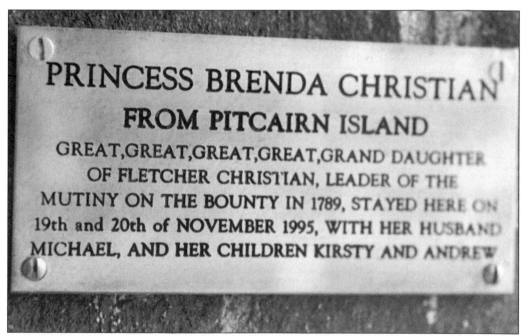

PRINCESS BRENDA CHRISTIAN FROM PITCAIRN ISLAND GREAT, GREAT, GREAT, GREAT, GRAND DAUGHTER OF FLETCHER CHRISTIAN, LEADER OF THE MUTINY ON THE BOUNTY IN 1789, STAYED HERE ON 19th and 20th of NOVEMBER 1995, WITH HER HUSBAND MICHAEL, AND HER CHILDREN KIRSTY AND ANDREW

Visits by Pitcairners to England are rare. Thus the visit by Brenda Christian and her family has been recorded for posterity by a brass plate on the house. The title 'Princess' is accorded because had she been the daughter of a 'chief' in Europe at the time of the mutiny, she would have had such a title.

Robert Lowry Young, known as 'Bobby', plays music on his gramophone in this 1930s photograph. Such historical musical instruments have long been replaced by tape recorders, compact discs and videos.

John Adams' gravestone. The original grave marker was of wood, covered with lead salvaged from the Bounty. It was replaced by this carved headstone that was sent out from England in the 1850s. John Adams' wife and daughter are buried in adjacent graves.

Great Yarmouth, England, 1995. Steve Christian and members of the George Prior Engineering Co. erect the portable frame carrying the navigation lights on the new longboat *Moss* then being built for Pitcairn Island. On the right of the picture is director MacLean who, at the time, he said later, was wondering whether or not to throw himself in the river!

Andrew, son of Brenda Christian, watches *Moss* being readied for the first of several test trips. The proving trials were satisfactory and the new longboat was delivered to Pitcairn Island shortly afterwards.

117

One quarter of the entire population of Pitcairn Island enjoying a picnic in the 1980s.

Pitcairn children of the 1950s, from left to right: Nancy Christian, Freda Christian, Marilyn Warren, Judy Warren, Beverly Warren, Julie Christian, Marlene Christian, Glen Clarke, Brian Young, Denis Christian, Barry Young and Ruby Warren.

This picture indicates the small area occupied by the Landing Place in Bounty Bay. The concrete landing stage, further extended since this photograph was taken, eases but does not eliminate the skill required to launch and land boats in anything but the calmest of seas. The Hill of Difficulty can be seen behind the boat sheds. When the mutineers landed in 1790 it was no more than a slippery goat track.

Typical Pitcairn home of the 1980s. The rooms are airy and well suited to the island way of life. Nearly every household has a workshop, with a bench, lathe and tools. The entire family may be involved in the process of carving, turning, sanding and finishing carvings.

The old: an islander looking at an early 'Message board' used to inform Pitcairners of the latest news.

The new: The radio station was established in 1938, but regular communications were not started until the 1940s. In 1952 additional short-wave facilities were introduced. A popular and affordable radio telephone service was implemented in 1985, allowing worldwide communication at a modest cost. This link was discontinued in 1992 and replaced by a 'high tech' satellite service, the high cost of which (call charges went up by 1,000%) makes its use prohibitive. The high cost has led to many islanders setting up amateur radio systems.

A plaque commemorating the birth place of Fletcher Christian at Moorland Close, Cockermouth, England. The plaque was commissioned and paid for by Bernard Christian-Bailey, a descendant now resident on Norfolk Island.

Adamstown, established by the original mutineers and named after the famous survivor. It is situated on a slope at the top of the Hill of Difficulty, several hundred feet above sea level. In the early days the mutineers were careful to ensure their village was well screened by trees, so that their houses could not be seen from passing ships.

Signpost indicating the directions of some of the island's main places and features. Although distances are not great, the steep paths and rough terrain can make walking tiring.

Quintal's Cavern. Many of the natural features on the island are named after the original mutineers. A notable absence has been the name of Quintal, but this has been rectified by the recent discovery of a hitherto hidden cavern by Ross Quintal while he was fishing from the rocky shore near Bounty Bay. The entrance is very small, but leads to a cavern. Both are natural, being caused by erosion. Steve Christian is seen coming out of the entrance.

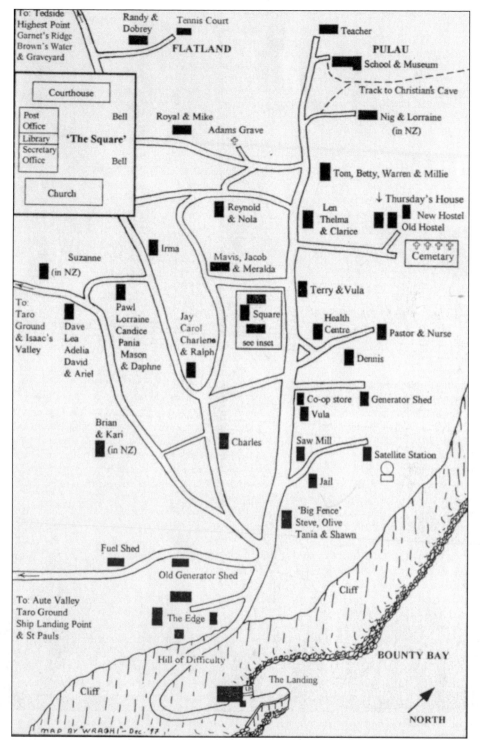

A map of Adamstown, included in the December 1997 issue of The Pitcairn Miscellany. The centre of public activities is 'The Square' in the centre. It is shown enlarged in the top left-hand corner.

PITCAIRN ISLAND POPULATION

When the *Bounty* arrived at Pitcairn in January 1790, it brought 28 people to populate the island:

Mutineers: Fletcher Christian, Alexander Smith (John Adams), Matthew Quintal, Isaac Martin, William Mills, Edward Young, John Mills, William Brown, John Williams.

Polynesian Men: Titahiti, Manarii, Teimua, Naiu, Tararo, Oha.

Polynesian Women: Mautua (Isabella), Faahotu, Mareva, Puarei, Teatuahitea, Teehuteatuaonoa, Teio, Teraura, Tevarua, Tinafanaea, Toofaiti, Vahineatua, Sully.

Population since 1790:

1790	28	1842	112	1857 7		1914 164E	1986 68
9 mutineers and		1843	116	Sailors from ship-		1916 164E	1987 59
19 polynesians		1844	121	wrecked *Wildwave*.		1924 183	1988 55
1808	35	1845	127	Make boat and leave		1934 202E	1989 55
1814	48	1846	134	1858 0		1936 200	1990 59
1819	44	1847	140	1859 16		1937 233E	1991 66
1825	66	1848	146	Two families return		1956 161	1992 *49
18.31: Jan 86		1849	155	from Norfolk Island		1960 144	1993 *46
March 0		1850	156	1864 47E		1961 126	1994 54
Population moved		1851	166	More Pitcairners		1966 96	1995 55
to Tahiti:		1852	168	return from Norfolk Is.		1968 76	1996 43
Sept 68		1853	172	1873 76		1970 91	1997 40
Pitcainers return		1855	187	1874 71E		1972 85	1998 66
from Tahiti		1856: Jan 193		1878 *89		1976 74	1999 46
1839	106	May 0		1884 92E		1979 61	2000 ?
1840	108	Population moved		1894 115		1982 55	
1841	111	to Norlfolk Island		1904 147E		1985 58	

E = Estimated   * = Census figures.   Last few years includes visitors.   Figures in ( ) = ages

Population at the time of 1993 Census:

Dave Brown (39)	Charlotte Christian (65)	Ron Christian(24)	Mavis Warren (56)	Royal Warren (65)
Lea Brown (32)	Irma Christian (66)	Suzanne Warren (34)	Meralda Warren (34)	Brian Young (39)
Adelia Brown (9)	Dennis Christian (38)	Jason Warren (7)	Jay Warren (37)	Kari Young (49)
David Brown (6)	Dobrey Christian (70)	Darrin Warren (4 mths)	Carol Warren (43)	Timothy Young (15)
Ariel Brown (2)	Steve Christian (42)	Tom Christian (58)	Charlene Warren (14)	Anette Young (11)
Len Brown (67)	Olive Christian (40)	Betty Christian (51)	Paul Warren (30)	Terry Young (35)
Thelma Brown (64)	Trent Christian (21)	Warren Christian (79)	Lorraine Warren (31)	
Clarice Brown (35)	Randy Christian (19)	Millie Christian (86)	Candice Warren (9)	
Janelle Brown (13)	Shawn Christian (18)	Daphne Warren (54)	Pania Warren (6)	
Charles Christian (64)	Tania Christian (15)	Jacob Warren (73)	Mason Warren (4)	

Islanders absent on Census Day:

Darlene Christian (16)	Reynold Warren (64)	Darralyn Warren (17)	Vula Young (65)
Sherilene Christian (18)	Nola Warren (52)		

Non permanent residents:

Mark Ellmoos (39)	Fritha Ellmoos (14)	Kai Ellmoos (8)	Gerrard Foley
Susan Ellmoos (39)	Obie Ellmoos (11)		Philippa Foley

This table shows that the current population of Pitcairn Island is not much bigger than the original colony established by the Bounty mutineers over 200 years ago, if temporary visitors are excluded. For most of the time the population has been much higher, reaching a peak of 233 in the mid-1930s. It is currently perilously low for an isolated community to thrive and a small number of carefully selected 'outsiders' are being allowed to set up residence to see if they can adapt to the island way of life. Men, rather than money, may determine the future of the island.

Seven
Facts and Figures

Physical Features

Pitcairn Island is a relatively small lump of rock rising above the Pacific Ocean, and appears to have been formed by volcanic activity. Most of its coastline consists of steep, inhospitable cliffs. Level land forms only about one-tenth of the total surface area, rolling land around one-third, steeply-sloping land another third and cliffs just over one-quarter. The relatively flat land in the centre slopes gently towards the settlement of Adamstown. There are a number of valleys, some only minor depressions caused by normal weathering. The lower slopes and floors of the valleys are covered with soil ideal for fruit trees.

Economy

Pitcairn Island earns its living in two distinct ways. Privately, the islanders make money by selling garden produce, carvings and basketwork, and by the export of dried fruit and honey. The public economy depends mainly on the sale of postage stamps, phone cards and coins to collectors, by far the biggest proportion coming from the sale of stamps.

Food

Although most vegetables and fruit are grown on the island, Pitcairners rely on the official 'supply ships' that come at least three times a year, bringing bulk foodstuffs such as flour, meat and canned food. Fish is very important to the Pitcairn diet, and the islanders do a great amount of fishing, either from rocks or from canoes. Sometimes public fishing trips are made using one of the longboats.

Vegetation

When the mutineers from the *Bounty* arrived at Pitcairn in 1790, the whole island was covered in trees. The need to clear land for crops, and wood for buildings, cooking and carvings, has left little today of the original forest. So, bushes and grass have taken its place. Early attempts to re-establish the forest were not successful, largely due to the destructive habits of the island's predatory goats. The goat problem has now been brought under control and replanting is proceeding. The shortage of wood means that supplies of the beautiful Miro tree, used for carving curios, now has to be collected by longboat from Henderson Island, over 100 miles away.

There is a variety of weeds and grasses on Pitcairn, with one weed, Lan, being a real problem, as its rapid growth enables it to take over cultivated areas. Flowers of Pitcairn are very pretty and are mainly of the tropical variety, such as Frangipani and Hibiscus.

Many fruits and vegetables grow well on the island, including bananas, coconuts, mangoes, lemons, guava, oranges, mandarins, paw-paw, limes, grapes and pineapples.

Transport

Up to the 1960s there were no vehicles on Pitcairn. There was only one means of getting about – walking. To move goods the Pitcairn wheelbarrow was developed in the nineteenth century. These had stub runners and hooked handles, to help on the steep and narrow tracks.

In 1965 two tractors were introduced, one with a bulldozer blade, which were used to convert the tracks and paths into narrow dirt roads. The roads encouraged some people to import a few motorbikes. In 1983 a bulldozer was airdropped by parachute that was used to further improve the roads. By 1999 there were twenty-one four-wheeled motorbikes, ten three-wheelers and one two-wheeler on the island.

Power

Public power is supplied by a diesel generator, and is generally available daily from 9 a.m. to 12 noon, and from 4 p.m. to 10 p.m. Many homes have privately owned generators, which can be used outside the public power times. Most homes have electric freezers, fridges, ovens and many other electric appliances, so the present diesel generating plant is heavily loaded.

Entertainment

Almost gone are the days of traditional film and game evenings, once so much a part of life on the island, as indeed is the case in most countries of the developed parts of the world. There is no television service, but videos are the major source of entertainment. Family picnics with fishing and diving activities are still popular, and two special days are celebrated each year – Christmas Day and Bounty Day.

Brenda Christian, a direct descendant of the chief mutineer, proudly displays a wooden model of the *Bounty* made by her grandfather. Pitcairners create many such magnificent carvings and curios, which are sold aboard visiting ships or by mail order.

Fish forms an important part of the Pitcairn diet and a large variety are caught for eating or trading. This picture is a postcard sent to the author, with the message 'Though the miles may lie between us and the distance may be far, you're very close in thought and heart, just as you always are.' Penned by Mavis Warren, this indicates that the current islanders have lost none of the inherent warm-heartedness of their Polynesian ancestors.

Pitcairn stamps are the island's main source of income and are eagerly sought after by collectors all over the world. A limited number of commemorative stamps are issued each year, making them affordable. After being on sale for one year, surplus stocks are burnt, as shown here.

★ IMPORTANT ANNOUNCEMENT ★

We have been asked by the **Pitcairn Police & Customs Officer** to make this announcement. Friends of Pitcairn and visitors to the island are asked **NOT** to send or bring **honey, other bee products, or used hive equipment or clothing** to Pitcairn. As many of you know, the Pitcairners have begun to expand their beekeeping efforts, and the island hives have recently been declared 100% free of disease. In order to keep the hives pristine, it is very important that the island not be accidentally exposed to products of bees from other areas that could contaminate the Pitcairn bee population. The Pitcairners and the bees thank you very much!

Pitcairn Honey: Nectar of the Pacific. A pure, natural product, the honey has a unique and rich flavour. The island is so small that the bees can choose from a variety of flowers that have pollen available for most of the year.

1.	3.

'Mɪᴅ the mighty Southern Ocean
  Stands an isolated rock,
Whiten'd by the surf's commotion,
  Riven by the lightning's shock.
	Ha! that flash yon grove illuming,
	  Long impervious to the sun;
	Now the quick report comes booming
	  From the ocean-rescued gun.

2.	**4.**

Hark! those strains to heaven ascending,
  From yon slopes of vivid green;
Old and young their voices blending,
  God preserve Britannia's Queen!
	List! the bell is gaily ringing,
	  Where a white-robed * train is seen!
	Now they all unite in singing
	  God preserve our gracious Queen!

This poem was composed by George Hunn-Nobbs, the nineteenth century pastor. In her book on the mutineers, published in 1870, Lady Belcher tells that the islanders had adapted the poem to the air of Rousseau's Dream and considered it to be their National Anthem.

A message mentioning Pitcairn Island inserted in the millenium issue of the British newspaper the *Daily Mail*.